The Good Citizen's Handbook

This book is dedicated to my grandparents: Dick and Bettye Reed, and Carmon and Alice McKnight—all model citizens. Thank you to my editor, Steve Mockus, and to designer Ben Shaykin, and the rest of the gang at Chronicle Books for giving me the opportunity to do this book and work with them again. Thanks, too, to my husband, Ian, and daughter, Esme, for allowing me to take over the dining-room table with stinky old books. And to my parents, Deborah and James Patrick, for always acting interested in my projects.

Library of Congress Cataloging-in-Publication Data available.

ISBN 0-8118-3066-7

Printed in Hong Kong.

Book design by Jennifer McKnight-Trontz

Distributed in Canada by Raincoast Books
9050 Shaughnessy Street
Vancouver, British Columbia V6P 6E5

10 9 8 7 6 5 4 3 2 1

Chronicle Books LLC
85 Second Street
San Francisco, California 94105

www.chroniclebooks.com

The Good Citizen's Handbook

A Guide to Proper Behavior

JENNIFER McKNIGHT-TRONTZ

CHRONICLE BOOKS
SAN FRANCISCO

Contents

Introduction

A GOOD CITIZEN is well-groomed and fun to be around. She's trustworthy, helpful, courteous, and kind. He's loyal, thrifty, clean, and brave. Good Citizens beware delinquency and obey even minor laws. They tend their yards, brush their teeth in a circular motion, vote in every election, and always try their best. They know, as R. O. Hughes points out in the 1930s textbook *Elementary Community Civics*, "The character of any community, however large or small, depends upon the character of its members. Every good citizen in the community is a good influence. Every evil citizen is a bad influence."

The Good Citizen's Handbook spells out everything you need to know to be a better person, in a healthy home and community, a strong country, and an ideal world. Culled from civics texts, citizenship manuals, government pamphlets, and scouting manuals from the 1920s to 1960s, the guidance in these pages recalls an optimistic nation, eager to put hand to heart for the "Pledge of Allegiance," knowing all the words and meaning them. It was a time when children might heed the advice of the 1925 primer *What to Do for Uncle Sam* without irony or question: "The Government says that you will be helping to grow into strong, useful citizens if you can learn to eat some of the things like the skin of the apple," and, "If each child in the United States stops to think whether he is wasting or saving for an hour each day, he will make the country richer for his efforts."

Today good citizenship means less to us. We worry far more about our demons than our duties. According to a 1995 *U.S. News and World Report* column by John Leo, entitled "The Unmaking of Civic Culture": "Starting in the 1960s, the nation's sense of itself has been deeply influenced by the rapid spread of therapies, encounter groups, self-help, the language of self-esteem and personal growth and an array of New Age notions, some of them quasi religions based on the primacy of self. . . .This culture of therapy has positioned itself as the antidote for America's fragmentation and the decline of civic culture." We belong to fewer civic groups, vote less, and spend far more time doing things by ourselves, for ourselves. No wonder it feels like everything's going to Hell.

The Good Citizen's Handbook is here to help. In "Good Citizenship Starts with You," we learn the importance of washing our hands before meals, a positive outlook, and not talking back. "Good Citizenship in the

Family" reveals the secrets of "right living." "Good Citizenship at School and Work" illustrates the value of school spirit, fair dealing, and proper penmanship. Chapters on citizenship in the neighborhood and community offer tips for turning blight into beauty, how to be friendly, and why we must never poison the neighbor's dog. "Good Citizenship in Your Country" ensures we fly the flag properly, and "Good Citizenship in the World" stresses that we must treat those from other countries as our neighbors, no matter how odd their beliefs may seem.

Good citizenship is our duty. The future depends on us. The alternative, as we are warned in Edwin C. Broome's and Edwin W. Adams' *Conduct and Citizenship*, is unthinkable: "Character is a nation's strength. The nations of the earth that, like the Roman Empire, have been overthrown were not defeated by outside enemies, but by their own failure to live up to high standards of national character."

—Jennifer McKnight-Trontz

1. Good Citizenship Starts with You

A Good Citizen Is Worthy

A GOOD CITIZEN IS—

1. A worthy man or woman, boy or girl—dutiful, devoted, obedient.

2. Well-informed and interested regarding the problems of his city, state, and nation. He takes advantage of every means to increase his knowledge of the needs of his city, his state, and his nation.

3. A worker—doing his full share in the work of his community, prompt and active in his cooperation with his fellows.

4. Zealous in his efforts to serve his city, his state, and his nation.

5. Healthy—keeping his body fit for service and helping his fellows do likewise.

6. Reverent—respecting the life, liberty, property, and feelings of others.

7. Concerned with the development of all that makes for beauty and happiness in the community of which he is a member.

8. Interested, not only in the production, but also in the conservation of the wealth of his country—provident, thrifty.

9. An active power for good in the political life of the community.

10. A good person—obedient, honest, trustworthy, kind, sympathetic, loyal—a good American.

REMEMBER that the American people have the greatest privileges and the most opportunities of any people in the world. But in order to enjoy these privileges and opportunities it is our first duty to make ourselves worthy of them.

A Good Citizen Is Well-Rounded

Your mental power is influenced by the kinds of nerve cells in your brain. These you have inherited from your parents. But if you do not take every opportunity to use and strengthen the

potential abilities with which you were born, they will never be as effective as they could be.

Unless you develop and make the best use of your brain, you will fall short of being the person you might have been. Your mental growth is affected by what you inherit and also by what you make of your inheritance.

A good citizen uses recreation to become a well-balanced and happy person.

The effective citizen has learned that the best kind of life is one that maintains a sensible proportion of work and play. He joins with others in parties, games, or other forms of recreation that give him a rest from workaday cares. He uses recreation not only for fun but to keep fit.

TIPS TO ENSURE THAT WORK DOES NOT DOMINATE YOUR LIFE
Read (a lot)
Take time each day to exercise, or join a sports team
Each week see at least one movie
Try a new recipe
Join a community organization

A Well-Rounded Life Promotes Good Mental Health

WORK

A job—or some regular, organized activity—is a "must" for most people. It gives us an outlet for our energies and helps us feel useful.

FRIENDS

Happy relationships with family, friends, and others around us make our lives richer and satisfy our need to feel loved and wanted and to be part of a group.

TALK

Expressing our upset feelings through safe channels helps relieve worry and tension. Talking things over with some trusted adult is one of the best ways of doing this.

PLAY

To be mentally healthy, we need to have fun. Some of us find our most enjoyable recreation in sports and games——others find pleasure and a sense of achievement in creative hobbies.

SPIRITUAL VALUES

Devotion to a religious faith helps keep a person mentally healthy. Everyone needs the strength that comes from knowing that there is order—and a power for good—in the universe, and that each one of us has a place and purpose in the scheme of things.

A Good Citizen Is Fun to Be Around

THE GOOD CITIZEN AND PLAY

In our play we are really a part of a play community just as in our homes we are a part of a home community. Each group in which we play is a real community during the time of the game. It is a group of people in a given place with common interests, playing the game according to certain rules.

- If leisure bears such an important relation to the health and well-being of each one of us, it certainly has a real relation to every one of the communities of which we are a part.

- If leisure makes us healthy and happier, then it also makes us better fit to do our share in each of the other communities. We will be better parents, better workers, better employees, better citizens, better scholars, better teachers, all because we have learned how to play.

PLANNING FOR THE BEST USE OF LEISURE

The question of what is the best use of leisure must be answered differently for each individual. The answer will depend upon his tastes, the opportunities available in his community, and the nature of his regular occupation. In general, however, our recreational needs are of the following types:

1. **OUTDOOR EXERCISE.** Except for those whose work provides outdoor exercise, most people need some recreation that will give them fresh air and exercise.

2. **SOCIAL CONTACT.** Recreations in which we associate with others of our own age and interests are important in developing friendliness, cooperation, and other qualities that enable one to get along successfully with other people. Games, dancing, and club activities provide this kind of recreation.

3. **CONSTRUCTIVE ACTIVITY.** Most of us like to be making something, whether it be a ship model, a dress, or a collection of stamps. Working at hobbies supplies recreation of this kind. Many people's hobbies involve a great deal of work, but this work is recreation for them because it is different from their regular occupations.

4. **MENTAL DIVERSION AND STIMULATION.** This kind of recreation may be obtained in a number of ways. Reading, listening to or playing music, seeing plays and moving pictures, all are examples.

A Good Citizen Is Healthy

Make a survey of your health practices by marking yourself *plus* or *minus* on each item in this Record.

1. Get up at a regular time every day.
2. Take a bath daily, a cold bath in the morning if the body reacts satisfactorily; warm cleansing baths at least twice a week.
3. Wash the hands before every meal.
4. Use an individual towel at all times.
5. Have your own comb and brush and keep your hair neat.
6. Brush the teeth thoroughly at least twice a day.
7. Have a bowel movement at a regular time every morning.
8. Wear clothing suitable to the weather and your activities.
9. Wear shoes of correct size and shape with rather low heels.
10. Drink plenty of water, four to six glasses daily.
11. Be on time for every meal.
12. Use plenty of time for each meal.
13. Eat slowly and chew food thoroughly.
14. Every day eat fruit at least once; potatoes and one other cooked vegetable; lettuce or some other green leafy vegetable.
15. Take at least two glasses of milk every day, as a beverage or in cooked food.

16. Drink no tea or coffee.
17. Eat candy and sweets only at the end of a meal.
18. Have, on the average, two hours of outdoor play or some form of vigorous exercise or work every day. If it is stormy, get some exercise indoors.
19. Keep good posture when sitting, standing, and walking.
20. Relax during the day; for instance, fifteen minutes after luncheon, and ten minutes before the evening meal.
21. Sleep nine or ten hours every night.
22. Have windows open in the bedroom at night.
23. Keep cheerful.
24. Try to see the best in the people you are with.
25. Treat others with courtesy.
26. Have a health examination annually, at school or elsewhere.
27. Twice a year have a dentist examine your teeth and do whatever is needed.
28. Be sure that your eyesight is normal or wear glasses if they are needed.
29. Protect yourself by means of vaccination.
30. Protect yourself by the preventive measures against diphtheria (the Schick Test and toxin-antitoxin).

A Good Citizen Avoids Infection

TO AVOID CATCHING AND SPREADING INFECTIONS

1. Avoid actual contact with people who have an infection, people who may be "getting" one, and people who have not fully recovered from one.

2. Keep far enough away from a person with a cold or any other nose, throat, or lung infection to avoid receiving the discharges from his coughing or sneezing.

3. Avoid using or even touching any articles (personal items, clothing, dishes, and the like) after they have been handled by a person with a disease.

4. Keep all articles out of the mouth that do not belong there. This includes pins, pencils, fingers, etc.

5. Keep hands clean by frequent washing. Be sure to wash the hands before eating, before preparing food or handling dishes, after going to the toilet, after touching pets or other animals, and after contact with a person who may be ill.

GOOD CITIZENSHIP

WRONG

A sneeze sends out
dust, dirt, or germs . . .

So...

RIGHT

Always hold a handkerchief

1. Breathe deeply of pure air.
2. Drink plenty of pure water.
3. Eat a sufficient quantity of pure, wholesome food.
4. Exercise daily in the open air.
5. Keep the body clean by frequent bathing.
6. Keep away from sources of contagious disease.
7. Secure a sufficient amount of rest.
8. Avoid worry.
9. Develop correct habits of posture.

STARTS WITH YOU

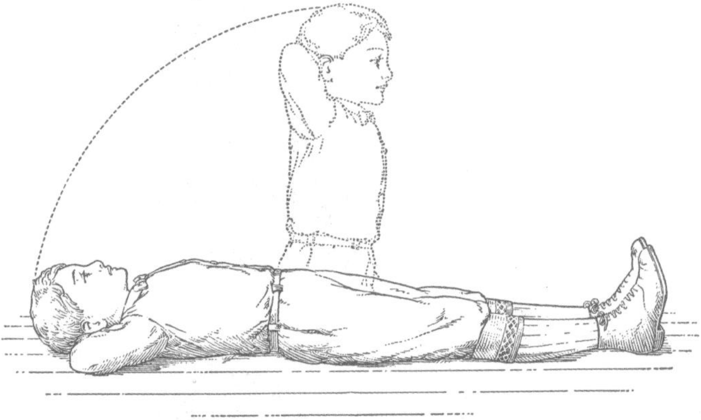

AN EXCELLENT KIND OF EXERCISE FOR THE ABDOMINAL MUSCLES

FITNESS PROGRESS CHART

Name_____

Pack_____ Medical Checkup_____
                                              (Date)

TEST	No. 1	No. 2	No. 3	No. 4	No. 5
DATE					
Pull-Ups					
Sit-Ups					
50-Yard Dash					
600-Yard Run (Walk)					
Standing Broad Jump					

GOOD CITIZENSHIP

A Good Citizen Is Fit

MILK + MEAT + VEGETABLES
+
FRUIT
=

CANDY + POP + CAKE ICE CREAM =

DON'T PEEL THE SKIN FROM THE APPLE BEFORE YOU EAT IT!

The Government says that you will be helping to grow into strong, useful citizens if you can learn to eat some of the things like the skin of an apple, that you always used to throw away. There are chemical properties, especially iron, in the skin of fruits that your bodies need. Try to eat at least one apple with its skin every day; drink a glass of milk; eat green foods in their season such as lettuce, spinach, dandelion greens, and green beans and peas.

A Good Citizen Eats Meat

Plenty of Meat

WRONG   **RIGHT**

Stretching is an excellent exercise for good posture if the body is kept in the correct position

A Good Citizen Stands Tall

Good Posture

A Good Citizen Controls Himself

Those who best control themselves can best serve their country.

• I will control my TONGUE, and will not allow it to speak mean, vulgar, or profane words.

• I will control my TEMPER, and will not get angry when people or things displease me.

• I will control my THOUGHTS, and will not allow a foolish wish to spoil a wise purpose.

THOUGHTFULNESS

a. What is thoughtfulness?
b. Why respect others?
c. How do we show this?
d. Where? When?

TREAT OTHERS WELL

a. What is good treatment?
b. Why should we treat others well?
c. How do we do this?
d. Whom should we treat well?
e. Do we benefit from treating others well?

A GOOD LITTLE BOY
NEVER
TALKS BACK

The Good Citizen Obeys the Law

The next time you are inclined to fret over or disregard a law, stop and think of the reason back of it. Then decide whether it is worth while to play the game of citizenship all the way by the rules.

The fellow who "fixes" a traffic ticket, hunts out of season, takes more fish than the limit allows, or dumps rubbish along the highway is undermining the democratic idea that ordinary citizens are intelligent enough to help govern themselves.

The good citizen has a proper respect for the law and obeys it. This is not because of a fear of what may happen to him if he breaks the law, but because he desires to do what is for the greatest good of all.

This citizen understands that even on a bicycle you must obey traffic laws.

2. Good Citizenship in the Family

Good Citizens in the Home

We cannot be good citizens of our nation unless we are good citizens of our home. Three key words to remember if we are to be good citizens of our home and nation: SERVICE, OBEDIENCE, and LOYALTY.

Unless the citizens in the home, as well as in the nation, are willing to work for other citizens, obey the rules, and are loyal, neither the home nor the nation can grow strong.

Remember: the home is the foundation of society; poor citizenship can usually be traced back to poor conduct or poor conditions at home.

IN EVERY WELL-ORDERED HOME THERE MUST BE CERTAIN RULES

One of the most important rules is for the time of all meals to be set. If we are not prompt in responding to the call for a meal we may delay the meal and cause an inconvenience to other members of the family.

The good son or daughter, mother or father, makes the good scholar, the good sportsman, the good worker, the good citizen. Anything that strikes at the home life of a nation strikes at the nation itself. The home and the family must be regarded as sacred if the safety of the state and the nation is to be secure.

IN THE FAMILY

Right Living

"Right Living" depends almost entirely upon what the individual thinks and does, and the home is the place where the fundamental principles of right and wrong are learned. So let us be careful about our life in the home, and carry out here the principles of good citizenship.

Your role as a family member is important

The family member in an American home who obeys, is careful with all that is bought for the home, and works with the family for its good and the welfare of the community, is just as much an American citizen as is a soldier who fights to protect the country.

KINDNESS, TRUTHFULNESS, HONESTY, COURTESY, AND CONSIDERATION for others are best learned in the home where these are the rule.

A boy or girl who acquires the wrong characteristics often has serious difficulty, later on, in trying to overcome them.

Be a Good Family Member

A good citizen starts out by being a good member of his family. The happiest families are those that do things together—things that all members of the family enjoy, like a tramp in the woods, a picnic, or a visit to some place of interest.

You don't have to go out of the house, though. Try taking turns reading aloud a book that would please everyone, like *Tom Sawyer;* or plan an evening of listening to and discussing fine music. The things you can do together are limitless.

IN A FAMILY THAT WORKS, worships, and plays together, the parents and children learn to consider and plan for the happiness of each other. Through family activities, children gain the self-esteem needed to get along in the real world.

The Family Together

Outdoor activities for family fun

- Going to a beach party or picnic.
- Spending the day in a park, forest preserve, wooded countryside, or the mountains.
- Taking part in outdoor sports, such as swimming, boating, fishing, etc.
- Visiting a nearby city for the day.
- Sightseeing in the community or in a nearby place.
- Attending parades, festivals, fairs, and carnivals.
- Taking a car trip.
- Taking part in special projects, such as gardening, bird feeding, bird watching, etc.
- Spending vacation days at a resort, at the shore, or in the mountains.
- Camping out for the weekend.
- Attending outdoor sports events, such as baseball and football games.

Special occasions the family may celebrate

Birthdays
Special achievements, awards, or recognitions of members
Graduations
Holidays
Mother's Day
Father's Day
Religious holidays
Special community holidays

Entertaining the Elderly

IDEAS FOR ACTIVITIES WITH ELDERLY PEOPLE

Find out what the aging person has wanted to do all his life but has never had time or opportunity to do, and encourage him to do it if possible.

Help him with outdoor activities such as gardening or fishing.

Secure for him the materials for creative efforts, such as woodworking, clay modeling, cartooning, painting, weaving, or knitting.

Help him to make up for education cut short in his youth by study of a foreign language or by guided reading.

Encourage him to join other older people for arts, crafts, games, and conversation in a recreation center or club.

Help him to take responsibility for some family duties, such as writing letters to relatives or keeping the accounts.

Help him to do some community volunteer work.

Rules for Family Safety

Safety checklist

You should have an emergency call list on or by your telephone. Be sure to include the family doctor, the nearest ambulance, fire station and police station, and the emergency offices or persons to call if something goes wrong with the water, gas, or electrical services in your home.

A GOOD CITIZEN CHECKS HIS HOME FOR THE FOLLOWING:

1. Are halls and stairs well lighted and free of things you might trip over?
2. Do all stairways have handrails?
3. Are stairtreads and porch steps in good repair?
4. Are rugs and carpeting skid-proof?
5. Are there safeguards against small children falling down stairs or out of windows?
6. Do bathtubs and showers have handholds and non-skid mats?
7. Are electric cords in repair and placed to prevent tripping?
8. Are cooking utensil handles turned away from edge of stove to prevent tipping?
9. Are window curtains kept away from stove?
10. Have chimney flues, furnace, gas pipes, electric circuits, and similar equipment been inspected recently enough to be considered safe?
11. Are basement, attic, and closets free of rubbish?
12. Are flammable fluids kept away from house, and oily rags disposed of?
13. Are poisonous materials marked and kept out of children's reach? Also matches?
14. Are firearms unloaded and locked up?
15. Are garage doors kept open when car motor is running?
16. Do you know what to do in case of fire in the home?

DO NOT play
around a stove.

DO NOT play
with medicines.

Ed Lafferty

DO NOT play
with electricity.

DO NOT stay out in
the sunshine too long.

DO NOT play
with matches.

Your Duties at Home

THINGS THAT MUST BE DONE REGULARLY

Have meals ready.
Have clothes ready.
Have the house clean and neat.
Care for the children.
Care for the plants.
Care for the pets.

Things that must be done occasionally

IN THE HOUSE Polishing floors, washing windows, changing screens or storm windows, shopping for needed household items, cleaning silver, fixtures, copper, etc.

OUT OF THE HOUSE Planting grass, pulling weeds, planting flowers, painting and cleaning exterior.

ERRANDS Grocery shopping, clothes and shoes buying, and paying bills.

TRADITIONAL AMERICAN HOME LIFE

RESTAURANTS MOVIES COMMERCIALIZED AMUSEMENTS DANCING SPORTS

CAN THE HOME HOLD ITS OWN?

Your Happy Family

The urge to get more and more luxuries consumes many Americans. In the "old days" the members of the family had very little in the way of luxuries or even comforts; they depended mainly on one another to make life happy and interesting. Today, we are more "gadget-minded." We tend to think less of human relations, and more of things that we can buy and use, often to impress other people. This has had its effect in weakening the home.

Think less of what the "Joneses" are doing or buying, and more about how to have a good time with your family without spending money. Think about what really makes you and your family happy—important things such as each other's company, a good story, exercise, and learning.

3. Good Citizenship at School and Work

The Good Citizen at School

ADVANTAGES OF EDUCATION TO YOU
1. Greater Earning Power Throughout Life.
2. More Useful Citizenship.
3. Better Use of Leisure Time.
4. Greater Enjoyment of Living.

A LESSON WORTH LEARNING

- OBEY SCHOOL RULES
- BE PROMPT
- ATTEND REGULARLY
- BE STUDIOUS
- SHOW RESPECT
- CONCENTRATE ON EVERY LESSON AS HARD AS YOU CAN
- DON'T WASTE PAPER OR PENCILS
- KEEP THE SCHOOL GROUNDS LOOKING WELL

In your school community, you have school laws or regulations. OBEY THEM! Do this not merely to keep out of trouble with the teachers. Do it because the regulations are made for the benefit of all the pupils.

It is also important that school citizens regularly complete their assigned school work. A bad school record will affect their future.

HINTS FOR GOOD SCHOOL CITIZENSHIP

1. Be loyal to your school. Learn its songs and cheers. Respect its traditions. Cooperate with your principal, teachers, and student leaders. Work constantly to improve your school. Help to eliminate its weaknesses, but don't talk it down.

2. Become familiar with school regulations and obey them. They are designed to help the school run smoothly and efficiently. If certain regulations seem unjust, work through your student leaders to present your case to the faculty.

3. Protect school property both for yourself and for those to follow you. Even if the artistic heart of a Michelangelo throbs beneath your sweater, do not carve on your desk your initials or "In memory of those who died waiting for the bell."

AT SCHOOL AND WORK

School Spirit

The laws of clean play

Clean play increases and trains one's strength, and helps one to be more useful to one's country. Therefore:

- I will not cheat, nor will I play for keeps or for money. If I should not play fair, the loser would lose the fun of the game, the winner would lose his self-respect, and the game itself would become a mean and often cruel business.

- I will treat my opponent with politeness.

- If I play in a group game, I will play, not for my own glory, but for the success of my team and the fun of the game.

- I will be a good loser or a generous winner.

GOOD CITIZENSHIP

A GOOD SCHOOL CITIZEN HAS
THE RIGHT KIND OF SCHOOL SPIRIT

School spirit is not easy to define, but when we speak of school spirit we use such words as PEP, LOYALTY, ENTHUSIASM, and SUCCESS.

The surest way to arouse school spirit is to get all of the pupils enthusiastically and loyally behind the interests and activities of the school. We usually associate athletics with school spirit. However, a pupil may show a fine spirit of loyalty to his school by excellent scholarship and commendable conduct and by speaking a good word for the school and its activities.

Student organizations

Student Council
Home-room organizations
Honor societies
Future Homemakers of America
Future Farmers of America
Junior Red Cross
Camera Club
Glee Club
Orchestra
Archery
Band, etc.

Penmanship Matters

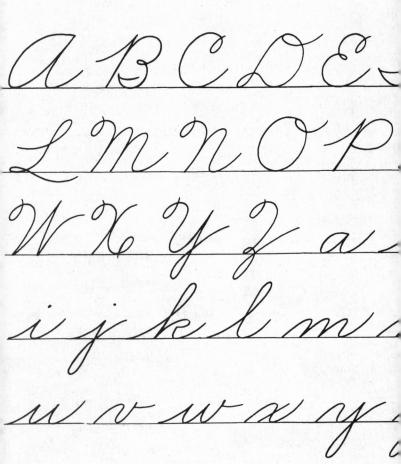

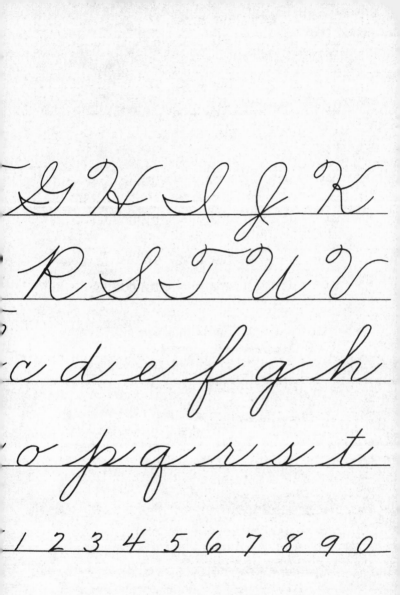

G H I J K

R S T U V

c d e f g h

o p q r s t

1 2 3 4 5 6 7 8 9 0

Play Fair

The businessman should play fair.
He should practice the square deal
toward those whom he employs, and
toward other businessmen. If he
does this, others will be benefited.
His employees will be rewarded
according to their efforts, and they in
turn will want to promote his business and his good name.

As citizens of any community we depend greatly upon other people and the products of their labor. If even one person stops doing his part, many others may be affected.

The intelligent business head has well ventilated and healthy workshops.

Health, Happiness, GOOD WORK
His employees feel better ; work better.

A factory should be supplied with

An Exhaust System.
Machinery, protected with wire guards.
A Ventilation System.
Fire Ladders and Fire Exits for emergencies.
Running water.
Lavatories.
Shower baths.
Water closets.
Plenty of Air and Light.
Space.   No overcrowding of work rooms.
A Sick Ward and Nurse.
A Dressing Room and a Rest Room.

EMPLOYEES' HEALTH

Everybody benefits by sanitary working conditions.

THE EMPLOYEE — Because he is in good health, contented and happy.

THE BOSS — Because his employees are in good health and turn out more and better work.

SOCIETY — Because prosperous and happy employees and employers are good citizens.

THE COUNTRY — Because co-operation between employer and employees makes the Country rich and powerful.

Good Workmanship

The laws of good workmanship

THE GOOD AMERICAN TRIES TO DO
THE RIGHT THING IN THE RIGHT WAY

The welfare of our country depends upon those who have learned to do in the right way the things that ought to be done.

• I will get the best possible education, and learn all that I can from those who have learned to do the right thing in the right way.

• I will take an interest in my work, and will not be satisfied with slipshod and merely passable work. A wheel or a rail or a nail carelessly made may cause the death of hundreds.

• I will try to do the right thing in the right way, even when no one else sees or praises me. But when I have done my best, I will not envy those who have done better, or have received larger reward. Envy spoils the work and the worker.

Your Best Effort

Employees take note of:
Thoroughness
Dependability
Accuracy
Technical skill
Neatness or orderliness of work
Amount of work accomplished
Speed
Judgment and common sense
Initiative and resourcefulness
Ability to work with and for others

The welfare of each individual, and of the nation, depends upon the way people work together or cooperate. More important than an individual's capacity to produce is his ability to cooperate with his coworkers.

1. I must be honest in the performance of my task, however humble or distinguished it may be.

2. I must be faithful in the performance of my tasks. Promptness in the performance of duties and the meeting of responsibilities is another form of faithfulness. I must be willing to do my full share of the work that falls to me, to pull my own weight in the boat.

3. I must be able to live peaceably with others. People who quarrel cannot work well together. I must be reasonable, willing to play fairly with my fellows, and, if necessary, to meet them more than half way in the interest of good will. Courtesy has been called the oil which prevents friction in society. If I am kindly disposed toward others, they are more likely to be kind to me.

4. I must be willing to follow the leadership and obey the commands of those who are in authority.

Teamwork

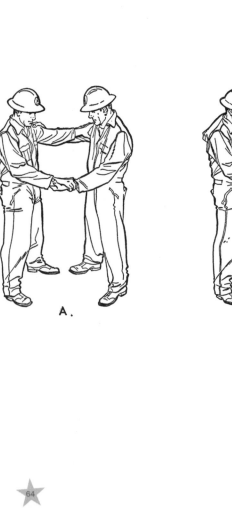

A.

B.

The laws of teamwork

THE GOOD AMERICAN WORKS IN FRIENDLY COOPERATION WITH HIS FELLOW WORKERS

One man alone could not build a city or a great railroad. One man alone would find it hard to build a house or a bridge. That I may have bread, men have sowed and reaped, men have made plows and threshers, men have built mills and mined coal, men have made stoves and kept stores. As we learn better how to work together, the welfare of our country is advanced.

- In whatever work I do with others, I will do my part and will help others do their part.

- I will keep in order the things which I use in my work. When things are out of place, they are often in the way, and sometimes they are hard to find. Disorder means confusion, and the waste of time and patience.

- In all my work with others, I will be cheerful. Cheerlessness depresses all the workers and injures all the work.

- When I have received money for my work, I will be neither a miser nor a spendthrift. I WILL SAVE OR SPEND AS ONE OF THE FRIENDLY WORKERS OF AMERICA.

4. Good Citizenship in the Neighborhood

Who Is a Neighbor?

The Pilgrim Fathers "got together" to come to this country. From other countries came groups which settled together at a "good bend in the crick."

Neighbors built cabins near each other, leaned on each other, worked with each other, protected each other.

Man has always liked someone else to talk to, someone else to walk with, to learn with, to worship with, to run races against, to wrestle, to argue politics with, and with whom to deplore the weather.

A neighborhood is a place to get together. All the people that live around you are your neighbors.

Being a good neighbor means more than just living near other people. It means being friendly and pleasant, or "neighborly."

Remember that we shouldn't stop being neighborly when we are away from our own neighborhood. We can be good neighbors to the people who live far away.

Ideas for getting neighbors together

FORM A NEIGHBORHOOD ASSOCIATION OR WATCH

HAVE A BLOCK PARTY

PRINT A NEIGHBORHOOD NEWSLETTER

HAVE A BAKE SALE FOR NEIGHBORHOOD IMPROVEMENTS

PLANT A NEIGHBORHOOD GARDEN

Be Friendly

How to make a new neighbor feel welcome:

✳ Smile pleasantly at a new neighbor

✳ Speak to the newcomer in a friendly
   fashion

✳ Invite the new neighbor over to your
   house for dinner

✳ Tell him or her about the community

✳ Invite the new neighbor to your club
   meetings

GOOD CITIZENSHIP

Belonging to a group

In order to be desirable members of any group we must be able to get along well with others. Have you ever thought about whether you are the kind of person that others like? Perhaps you sometimes feel that members of your groups do not welcome you to their activities as cordially as you would like. Have you ever tried to understand why you have this feeling, or to see what you could do to make people like you better?

We know that some ways of behaving cause people to be liked by others. Look at this list:

We usually like a person who
    1. does his share when there is work to do.
    2. is willing to listen to the suggestions of others.

We also know that some people do certain things that others dislike. Look at this list:

A person is usually disliked if he
    1. loses his temper when he doesn't win.
    2. is always boasting.

Tend to Your Home

TO MAKE YOUR NEIGHBORHOOD ATTRACTIVE, BEGIN
FIRST WITH YOUR HOME. If people have homes that
are in good taste and arranged attractively, they will
not be satisfied with dirty, carelessly kept streets and
buildings.

If all the families on a street agreed to clean up
their property, and keep the sidewalks swept and
their lawns in order, the result would be a street
which would be a credit to any neighborhood.

IF ONE PERSON DOES NOT LIVE UP TO HIS
AGREEMENT, THE EFFECT OF THE WHOLE PLAN IS
SPOILED.

A BEAUTIFUL TOWN IS THAT ONE IN WHICH EVERY FAMILY MAKES ITS OWN HOME BEAUTIFUL. Get out your tool box and your paint pot, and mend the pickets in the fence and put new screws into the gate hinge. Paint the fences, too.

Rake up the straw and leaves in front of the house and tie these up in papers or an old sack for burning.

Perhaps you can put a fresh coat of paint on the window boxes outside of the living room, and get rich earth for them in which nasturtiums or pansies will thrive and blossom all summer.

Rake the gravel walk that leads from the gate to the front door, and sweep the sidewalk in front of your house every day.

Turn Blight into Beauty

Signs of blight to look for in the neighborhood

- Cracked masonry walls and foundations, loose bricks, paint peeling off, splintered window sills and frames.
- Rusted down spouts, leaking roofs, loose shingles.
- Old homes converted to rooming houses.
- Broken sidewalks and rough streets.
- Porches and steps in need of repair.
- Trash piled up at doorways.
- Soiled curtains at windows.

Sometimes the appearance of a neighborhood is spoiled by an ugly vacant lot. This is especially true if the people of the neighborhood are accustomed to throwing their rubbish onto the lot. If the community can secure permission from the owner of the lot to have a community garden, the results are remarkable.

Street lighting has a big place in the attractiveness of a city. In the first place, a well-lighted street does not encourage crime and law breaking as a dark street does. Our bright thoroughfares tend to make us feel safe when we are out at night. Ornamental lampposts are beautiful as well as useful.

As good citizens we shall try to cultivate the habit of refraining from doing anything that will mar even the appearance of our streets.

A Friendly and Pleasant Neighborhood

GOOD CITIZENSHIP

IN THE NEIGHBORHOOD

IT IS NOT RIGHT TO LEAVE POISON ABOUT FOR CATS OR DOGS, or to abandon a horse, a dog, or a cat that is diseased or dying. This is not only cruel to the animal itself but puts other animals in danger.

Watch, too, for any person who drops glass, nails, pieces of metal, or any substance that might wound or injure an animal on the public roads.

Don't kill or wound or hurt any bird, deer, squirrel, rabbit, or any other animal.

Don't take away the animal's young, or birds' eggs, or sell, or knowingly buy any birds or animals that have been so taken.

Animals Bring Love and Happiness

GOOD CITIZENSHIP

The Good Neighbor

1. Always knock before you enter someone's home.

2. Say hello and goodbye when you see a neighbor.

3. Offer your help when a neighbor needs it.

4. Keep an eye on a neighbor's home when they are away.

5. Don't play music too loud, especially if you live in an apartment building.

6. Do not work on your car in the driveway for more than a few hours a week.

7. Keep your home as attractive as possible, painting and landscaping regularly.

Armed and Safe

DO THE FOLLOWING to keep the home and neighborhood safe from wrong doers:

✓ Make sure all streetlights are working properly.
✓ Keep hedges trimmed around your house.
✓ Lock windows and doors even when you are home.
✓ Get to know the police officers responsible for your area.
✓ Post Neighborhood Watch signs throughout the neighborhood.

GOOD CITIZENSHIP

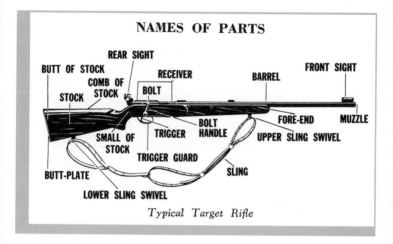

NAMES OF PARTS

Typical Target Rifle

If you own a gun:

1. Treat every gun as if it were loaded until you personally have proven otherwise.

2. Keep the gun locked and out of the reach of children.

3. Never handle a gun if you have been drinking alcohol.

5. Good Citizenship in the Community

WHY WE LIVE IN GROUPS

People live in groups because there are advantages in doing so. By combining their efforts, members of a community are able to accomplish many things that could not be accomplished by persons working individually. By acting as a group and making contributions to a common fund, the members are able to appoint particular individuals or groups to perform the many services that are necessary to the welfare of the community. Such services as police protection could not be performed, or would be performed less efficiently and economically, if each individual acted for himself.

Many of our proudest achievements are the result of the cooperation of many individuals in a group. No towering skyscraper could have risen because of the efforts of one man. No man alone could have built the Golden Gate Bridge or the tunnels that make it possible for men to drive their cars beneath the Hudson River.

A Heart
for
Hospitality

A Community of Good Citizens

What constitutes a community? Any group of people, living or working or playing together in a given place, with common interests and common laws, for a common end, constitutes a community.

We are all members of many communities:

School
Place of Worship
Work
Our town and state
Our country, the United States
The world

Our home and family are bound together by the strongest of common interests, love.

Remember: the same conduct which is necessary to a good member of your family or your work, is needed to become a good citizen of your local community, your state, or your nation. Good conduct and good citizenship are the same. The faithful performance of our daily tasks, whether in the home, the school, or in any of the larger communities, is a real test of our citizenship.

ALCOHOL

The **DRUNKARD** is subject to
Tuberculosis, Venereal Diseases,
Delirium Tremens, General Debility.

The DRUNKARD has children threatened with
Tuberculosis, Rickets, Insanity, Epilepsy.

ALCOHOLISM
MEANS DEATH TO THE NATION

Responsibility

The community's responsibility

In every community there are some people who not only contribute nothing to the progress of the community, but have to be cared for by it. These are sometimes spoken of as the dependent and the delinquent. The dependent include the aged, the poor people, the sick, and the children. The delinquent are those who have gone astray from the right path and have violated the laws or established customs of the community. All these people must be cared for by the community, so that they may not harm themselves or others.

Causes

There are many causes of poverty, and it exists in nearly every community. Old age makes others unable to work. Plain laziness is the trouble with many. Extravagance and poor management account for many others. Bad habits like gambling also have brought disaster to many families.

Whatever the reasons, it is better for the community to bear the burden of the poor and unfortunate and help them as much as possible.

Be a Part of It

Join any number of local clubs in your community. Everyone is happier if he feels he is a part of something. People need to feel that they really belong to their family, their school, their church, neighborhood, and community. People who feel left out of things become unhappy, even though their needs have been met. We all feel the need to "belong."

By taking the initiative and getting acquainted with your community and its various organizations, you will uncover plenty of civic work waiting to be done.

While cooperating on a community project, you will associate with a high type of public-spirited people.

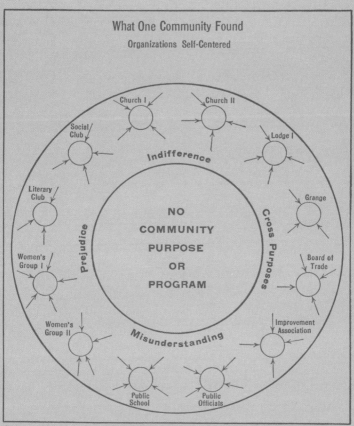

What One Community Found

Organizations Self-Centered

Church I — Church II — Lodge I

Social Club — *Indifference* — Grange

Literary Club — *Prejudice* — NO COMMUNITY PURPOSE OR PROGRAM — *Cross Purposes* — Board of Trade

Women's Group I — Improvement Association

Women's Group II — *Misunderstanding* — Public Officials

Public School

Courtesy of Massachusetts Agricultural College, The Extension Service, Community Organization

A divided community

This drawing represents the situation of a community lacking unity, purpose, and pride. As the arrows suggest, each organization makes its plans without any regard for the interests of the community as a whole. Make a similar drawing showing the organizations mentioned above in a relationship that has been prompted by unity, purpose, and pride.

REMEMBER: If there is something wrong with one part, even a tiny part, of a machine, it affects the working of the whole thing, and we take care to have it fixed right away.

What You Owe the Community

THINK IN TERMS OF THE WHOLE COMMUNITY
not only of your own section in it. Desire good houses for all
the citizens, good schools for all the children, and good
places to play for all children and not just your own.

A major benefit of community recreation is the development of a desirable community spirit, sometimes called
morale.

Wherever people act together in groups, their interest
and pride in local affairs tends to increase. This interest and
pride often brings about changes which benefit the whole
community and make it a better place in which to live.

THE VIEWS AND FEELINGS OF ONE PERSON
added to those of his neighbor and the neighbors of both
constitute what we call *public opinion* in a community. It is
public opinion that determines whether a community shall
be progressive and try to improve itself or be satisfied to do
as little as possible for the benefit of its citizens. Every person has his place, and the community whose doctrine is "one
for all, and all for one" is the community that is going to do
the most work for its members and for other communities.
Each individual should do his part to promote the good of
the whole.

Community Spirit

People are likely, once in a while, to get discouraged about the community in which they live. A good cure for that state of affairs is to take a kind of inventory that will show just what the community is doing for the people who really form the community. In almost every case the inventory adds up to more than was thought. Probably your community does more for you than you are aware.

One of the best services your community may offer is a library; visit it often.

EXAMPLES OF POOR COMMUNITY SPIRIT

What the community may offer:

Places of worship
Schools
Museums
Concerts
Theaters
Youth centers
Libraries
Playgrounds and parks
Beaches and swimming pools
Art galleries
Fairs and exhibitions
Zoos

The Problem of Delinquency

ORGANIZED RECREATIONAL PROGRAM GOING ON

SPORTS — MUSIC — HOBBIES
DANCING — DISCUSSIONS
ARTS AND CRAFTS
Expert Supervision

ALL TEEN-AGERS WELCOME

JUVENILE DELINQUENCY

COMMUNITY RECREATIONAL PLANNING

ONE ANSWER TO JUVENILE DELINQUENCY

WRONG DOERS

Unfortunately, in practically every community there are some people who are unwilling to cooperate with their fellows. Not only are they unwilling to cooperate, but they deliberately do things which the people of their own group have determined must not be done.

Remember that the best way to reduce crime is to prevent it by proper methods of training at home and at school; and that the best way to deal with criminals is to make good citizens of them.

WHEN WE DO WRONG

Sin: An act contrary to a person's conscience.

Vice: An act harmful to a person's health or morals.

Crime: An act that breaks the law.

HOW TO PLANT
A TREE OR SHRUB

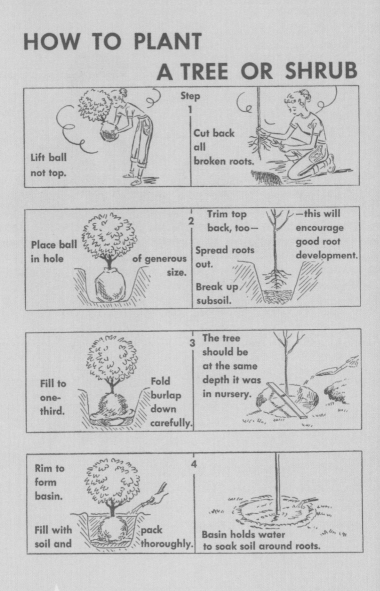

Lift ball not top.

Step 1

Cut back all broken roots.

Place ball in hole of generous size.

2

Trim top back, too— —this will encourage good root development.

Spread roots out.

Break up subsoil.

Fill to one-third.

Fold burlap down carefully.

3

The tree should be at the same depth it was in nursery.

Rim to form basin.

Fill with soil and pack thoroughly.

4

Basin holds water to soak soil around roots.

Care for Your Surroundings

CORRECT

You Must Abide by the Law

Often the presence of a policeman will keep a person from committing a crime.

THE SAFETY OF A COMMUNITY depends upon the honesty and efficiency of its police force. It is not enough that policemen should have respect for the laws they enforce; they should also discharge their duties in such a manner that the public will have respect for the laws.

Law-enforcement agencies protect the rights of individuals. In the U.S., everyone has certain fundamental rights that are guaranteed in the federal Constitution and in the state constitutions.

Because of police we are able to feel reasonably secure, in our homes and on the streets, against robbery and violence.

Besides combating crime, policemen direct traffic and maintain order in public places.

Driving for the Common Good

THE LIFE YOU SAVE MAY BELONG TO SOMEONE ELSE

When you operate a motor vehicle, you are responsible for *everyone* on the highway!
This is a responsibility only a mature-minded person can assume.
The good driver realizes that traffic regulations are set up for the safety of all and for compliance
by all. Running stop signs, over-speeding the limits, cutting in and out of traffic,
only prove that the person behind the wheel hasn't grown out of the pampered baby stage.
You're not "with it" if you believe you are a privileged character with a car!

YOU CAN WIN NEW FRIENDS AND INFLUENCE OTHERS

Have you ever noticed that "solid citizen" who, while driving, lets the other fellow go first, signals his turns, or otherwise extends courtesy to total strangers? You'll be the first to admit that it made you feel good when another driver was courteous to you . . . so show your good manners, and you'll give all teen-age drivers a boost. It will prove contagious.

6. Good Citizenship in Your Country

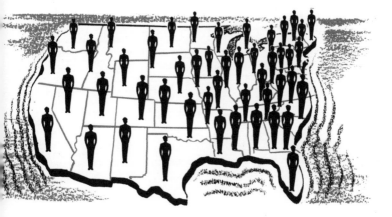

Be Happy to Pay Your Taxes

Cigarettes or a better government?

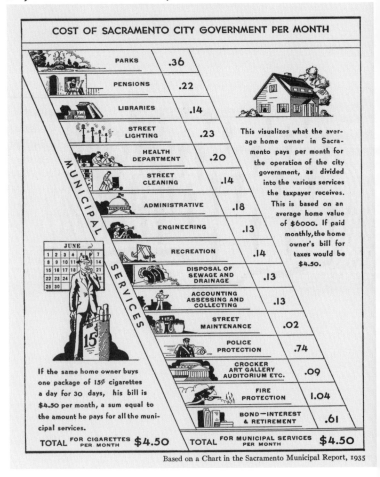

COST OF SACRAMENTO CITY GOVERNMENT PER MONTH

Service	Cost
PARKS	.36
PENSIONS	.22
LIBRARIES	.14
STREET LIGHTING	.23
HEALTH DEPARTMENT	.20
STREET CLEANING	.14
ADMINISTRATIVE	.18
ENGINEERING	.13
RECREATION	.14
DISPOSAL OF SEWAGE AND DRAINAGE	.13
ACCOUNTING ASSESSING AND COLLECTING	.13
STREET MAINTENANCE	.02
POLICE PROTECTION	.74
CROCKER ART GALLERY AUDITORIUM ETC.	.09
FIRE PROTECTION	1.04
BOND—INTEREST & RETIREMENT	.61

This visualizes what the average home owner in Sacramento pays per month for the operation of the city government, as divided into the various services the taxpayer receives. This is based on an average home value of $6000. If paid monthly, the home owner's bill for taxes would be $4.50.

If the same home owner buys one package of 15¢ cigarettes a day for 30 days, his bill is $4.50 per month, a sum equal to the amount he pays for all the municipal services.

TOTAL FOR CIGARETTES PER MONTH **$4.50**

TOTAL FOR MUNICIPAL SERVICES PER MONTH **$4.50**

Based on a Chart in the Sacramento Municipal Report, 1935

Where taxes come from:
Sales taxes
Gasoline taxes
Motor taxes
Licenses and fees
Income taxes
Estate and gift taxes
Payroll taxes

Where the money goes:
Education
Police and fire department
Water sanitation
Health department
Libraries
Welfare and relief
Highways

- Taxes are a way to share the expense of government.
- A good tax is a fair way of dividing that expense.
- The money government spends is the people's money.
- We have set up safeguards to make sure the people's money is spent honestly.
- It is the business of our officials to see that the money is spent wisely.

EDUCATION

POLICE AND COURTS

FIRE PROTECTION

STREET LIGHTING

PUBLIC HEALTH

RECREATION

IN YOUR COUNTRY

107

Make Your Ballot Count

*S*o you're going to
Vote!

The very first duty of every citizen of voting age is to become a voter. When you first become a voter, you will probably be asked whether you wish to enroll in a political party. Many voters do not want to do this. Either they are not interested in politics, or they wish to be "independent"—that is, not bound to a political party. The only choice you must make is what or whom to vote for.

Many people feel their vote is insignificant among the millions of votes cast. This is not true. A change of just one vote in each precinct would have reversed the outcome of many elections, not only at state and local level, but congressional and presidential contests as well.

When we criticize our government and political leaders for high taxes, inflation, or laxity in law enforcement, we criticize ourselves. *We make the laws under which we live.* By voting or failing to vote we elect our leaders to public office.

These marks are legal

In each case a cross has been used and the intersection of the lines of the cross is inside the circle or square.

These markings apply to the circle at the head of the ticket or the squares for the individual candidates.

These spoil your ballot

Invalid because crosses were not used.

Void because the lines of the cross do not intersect within the square.

Jury Duty Is Your Duty

WHEN YOU RECEIVE A NOTICE of jury duty, your first reaction may be, "Brother, how can I get out of this?" It interferes with your work or leisure. It's a lot of trouble. The pay is chicken feed.

Yet anyone who dodges responsibility of jury duty digs his little spadeful away from the foundation of one of our country's broadest freedoms.

A jury of twelve impartial, open-minded men and women, a little cross section of the community, under oath, is every man's protection against injustice, individual prejudice, intolerance, and persecution.

Therefore, when our busiest, most responsible, and mostly intelligent citizens avoid jury duty, one of our greatest liberties starts falling apart.

JUSTICE

Government Is the Will of the People

We are responsible for our government. When we are talking about the government we must remember that we are talking about something of which we ourselves are a part.

The Constitution begins with "We, the people"; this includes each and every one of us. When we talk about what the government does for us we are really talking about what we are doing for ourselves.

WHO, ME?

Yes, you some day may be asked to run for office — as councilman, mayor, state representative, alderman or some other office. When that time comes, remember: if desirable citizens refuse when their fellow citizens ask them to be a candidate for office we will be governed more and more by people who have their own axes to grind.

★ ★ ★ ★ ★ ★ ★ ★ ★

WHAT DO YOU KNOW ABOUT YOUR STATE GOVERNMENT?

A. What is the legislative body called?
   1. What are the names of its chambers?
   2. How are its members elected and for what terms?
   3. How much are they paid?
   4. How often does the legislature meet?
   5. What are its principal duties?
   6. What are the limitations on its powers?

B. Who is the governor?
   1. What qualifications must he have?
   2. What is his term of office?
   3. What are his principal duties?
   4. What are his powers and limitations on them?
   5. How much is he paid?

C. What is the State's highest court called?
   1. How many members does it have?
   2. How are they chosen and for what terms?
   3. How much are they paid?
   4. What are the court's principal duties?

D. What department or other division of your state government is concerned with each of the following?

Schools	Highways
Public health	Prisons
Social welfare	Budgeting
Agriculture	Auto registration
Conservation	State militia
Labor	Tax collection
Commerce	Law enforcement
Public works	

★ ★ ★ ★ ★ ★ ★ ★ ★

A Lobby of One

FORMS OF ADDRESS

To the President	The President The White House Washington 25, D. C. My dear Mr. President: I have the honor to.... Respectfully yours,
To Cabinet Officer	The Honorable......... The Secretary of........ Washington 25, D. C. My dear Mr. Secretary (or Madam Secretary):.... Sincerely yours,
To a U. S. Senator	Hon................... United States Senate Washington 25, D. C. My dear Senator:....... Sincerely yours,
To a U.S. Congress-man	Hon. .... House of Representatives Washington 25, D. C. My dear Congressman (Congresswoman*):...
To a Governor	Hon................... Governor of........... (Name of State Capital City) My dear Governor: (or Dear Sir or Madam:)

To a State Senator or Representative	Hon...................
	The State Senate
	(Name of State Capital
	  City)
	Dear Sir (or Madam):....
	(or My dear Mr., Miss or
	  Mrs...............:)

To a Mayor	Hon................... Mayor of the City of..... (City and State) Dear Sir (or Madam) (or My dear Mayor...:)

The term "Congressman" seems likely to become general for both men and women, like "chairman."

Whenever you have a question to ask, a complaint to make, or an idea to express, it is your democratic privilege to write a letter to a public official telling him or her how it looks to you and why. Such a letter, if courteous, thoughtful and to the point, can exert influence.

The Pledge of Allegiance

DISPLAYING THE FLAG

When carried in a procession with another flag or flags, the Flag of U. S. A. should be in the (1) on the marching right, (2) when there is a line of other flags, the Flag of U. S. A. should be in the front of the center of that line.

When grouped with other flags (state flags, pennants of societies, etc.), the Flag of U.S.A. should be at center or at highest point.

When displayed with another flag against a wall with crossed staffs the Flag of U. S. A. should be on flag's own right and its staff should be in front.

When displayed over middle of street the Flag should be suspended vertically with stars to north in an east and west street, or to the east in a north and south street.

When displayed from staff projecting from window or building, stars should go clear to peak of staff (unless at half staff).

When Flag is suspended over sidewalk from a rope extending from a building to a pole, it should be hoisted out from the building towards the pole, stars first.

When displayed in a manner other than on staff or rope (as shown above), the Flag should always be displayed flat, whether indoors or out. The stars should be uppermost and to the Flag's right (your left). It should be shown in a window in the same manner, that is, the stars should be at the left of the observer in the street.

When festoons, rosettes or drapings are desired, use red, white and blue bunting, *but never the Flag.*

When flags of states or cities or pennants of societies are flown on the same halyard, the Flag of U. S. A. should always be at the peak. When flown from adjacent staffs the Flag of U.S.A. should be hoisted first and lowered last. In such a case, no other flag or pennant should be placed at the right of the Flag of U. S. A., that is, to the observer's left.

When flown at half staff the Flag should be hoisted to the peak for an instant, then lowered to the half-staff position, but before lowering the Flag for the day it should be raised again to the peak.

When flags of two or more nations are displayed they should be flown from separate staffs of the same height and the flags should be approximately equal size. International usage forbids the display of the flag of one nation above that of another in time of peace.

Bunting of the national colors should be arranged with the blue at the top.

When used on a speakers' platform, the Flag, if displayed flat, should be above and behind the speaker. If flown from a staff it should be at the speaker's right. It should never be used to cover the speaker's desk nor to drape over the front of the platform.

When displayed in church—(1) In body of church the Flag should be on staff in position of honor at congregation's right as it faces the clergyman. (2) If in a chancel or on a platform the Flag should be on the clergyman's right, as he faces the congregation.

When worn as a badge, the Flag should be small and without folds. It should be pinned to the left breast of dress or coat or to the left coat lapel. It must not be used as a part of a costume or as a decoration.

No advertising or lettering may appear upon it. The Flag as a trade-mark for merchandise is prohibited by law. No advertising sign should be fastened to a pole from which the Flag is flown.

Do not use the Flag as a portion of a costume or athletic uniform. Do not put on cushions, handkerchiefs or boxes.

GOOD CITIZENSHIP

I pledge allegiance to the Flag
of the United States of America,
and to the Republic for which it stands,
one Nation, under God, indivisible,
with liberty and justice for all.

GOOD CITIZENSHIP

Your Duty

THE GOOD AMERICAN DOES HIS DUTY

The shirker or the willing idler lives upon the labor of others; burdens others with the work which he ought to do himself. He harms his fellow citizens, and so harms his country.

> I will try to find out what my duty is—what I ought to do; and my duty I will do, whether it is easy or hard. What I ought to do I can do.

HOW TO REGISTER FOR THE DRAFT

✪ Determine whether you must register. All male citizens and aliens must register within 30 days after their 18th birthday. Exceptions include those already on active duty with the armed forces and nonimmigrant aliens.

✪ Determine where you should go to register. You can register for the draft at any United States post office.

✪ Complete a registration form. The form will ask for such information as your name, address, sex, date of birth, social security number, and current telephone number.

✪ Date and sign the form in the presence of a clerk at the post office. Be sure to use ink on the form.

Fundamentals

Code of the Junior Rifleman

1. I will cock my gun and pull the trigger only when I am aiming at the target which I intend to shoot.

2. I will unload my gun and open the action as soon as I finish shooting and before I move from the firing line.

3. I will immediately make sure that any gun I handle is not loaded.

4. I will shoot only on a safe rifle range or, if hunting, only at legal game in places where persons and property are not endangered.

5. I will unload and open my gun before I climb a tree, fence, or similar obstacle.

6. I will remember that a .22 caliber bullet will travel for one mile; that it will go through nine inches of ordinary board; and that it will riccochet (glance) a long way across water.

7. I will "play it safe" at any time when I am in doubt of the proper action with a gun.

8. I will see that every one around me obeys these rules for the safety and good of all.

9. I will give my help to any less skillful shooter and will seek the advice of better marksmen for myself.

10. I will do my part to make America, once again, "A Nation of Riflemen".

GOOD CITIZENSHIP

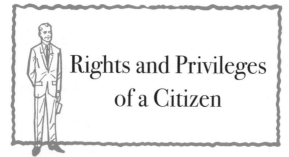

Rights and Privileges of a Citizen

1. I may think as I please.

2. I may speak or write as I please, so long as I do not interfere with the rights of others.

3. I have the right to vote. By my vote I choose the public officers who are really my servants.

4. I have the right to choose my work, to seek any job for which my experience and ability have fitted me.

5. I have the right to try to improve my lot through various means.

6. I have the right to a prompt trial by jury, if I should be accused of a crime.

7. I may seek justice in the courts where I have equal rights with others.

8. I have the privilege of sharing in the benefits of many of the natural resources of my country.

9. I have the right to worship as I think best.

10. I have the right to "life, liberty, and the pursuit of happiness."

The Constitution Is Your Business

We the People

Article I

Know Your Constitution

FROM THE CONSTITUTION
OF THE UNITED STATES OF AMERICA

PREAMBLE

 WE the People of the United States, in Order to form a more perfect Union, establish Justice, insure domestic Tranquility, provide for the common defence, promote the general Welfare, and secure the Blessings of Liberty to ourselves and our Posterity, do ordain and establish this Constitution for the United States of America.

THE BILL OF RIGHTS

The first ten amendments to the Constitution:

ARTICLE I

Congress shall make no law respecting an establishment of religion, or prohibiting the free exercise thereof; or abridging the freedom of speech, or of the press; or the right of the peop'e peaceably to assemble, and to petition the Government for a redress of grievances.

ARTICLE II

A well regulated Militia, being necessary to the security of a free State, the right of the people to keep and bear Arms, shall not be infringed.

ARTICLE III

No Soldier shall, in time of peace be quartered in any house, without the consent of the Owner, nor in time of war, but in a manner to be prescribed by law.

ARTICLE IV

The right of the people to be secure in their persons, houses, papers, and effects, against unreasonable searches and seizures, shall not be violated, and no Warrants shall issue, but upon probable cause, supported by Oath or affirmation, and particularly describing the place to be searched, and the persons or things to be seized.

ARTICLE V

No person shall be held to answer for a capital, or otherwise infamous crime, unless on a presentment or indictment of a Grand Jury, except in cases arising in the land or naval forces, or in the Militia, when in actual service in time of War or public danger; nor shall any person be subject for the same offence to be twice put in jeopardy of life or limb; nor shall be compelled in any criminal case to be a witness against himself, nor be deprived of life, liberty, or property, without due process of law; nor shall private property be taken for public use, without just compensation.

ARTICLE VI

In all criminal prosecutions, the accused shall enjoy the right to a speedy and public trial, by an impartial jury of the State and district wherein the crime shall have been committed, which district shall have been previously ascertained by law, and to be informed of the nature and cause of the accusation; to be confronted with the witnesses against him; to have compulsory process for obtaining witnesses in his favor, and to have the Assistance of Counsel for his defence.

ARTICLE VII

In Suits at common law, where the value in controversy shall exceed twenty dollars, the right of trial by jury shall be preserved, and no fact tried by a jury, shall be otherwise re-examined in any Court of the United States, than according to the rules of the common law.

ARTICLE VIII

Excessive bail shall not be required, nor excessive fines imposed, nor cruel and unusual punishments inflicted.

ARTICLE IX

The enumeration in the Constitution, of certain rights, shall not be construed to deny or disparage others retained by the people.

ARTICLE X

The powers not delegated to the United States by the Constitution, nor prohibited by it to the States, are reserved to the States respectively, or to the people.

Know Your History

SOME IMPORTANT DATES:

1776..... *Declaration of Independence signed.*

1783..... *Treaty of Paris ends American Revolution, Independence recognized.*

1788..... *U.S. Constitution is adopted.*

1789..... *George Washington becomes the first president.*

The Star-Spangled Banner

O say can you see by the dawn's early light
What so proudly we hail'd at the twilight's last gleaming,
Whose broad stripes and bright stars through the perilous **fight**
O'er the ramparts we watch'd, were so gallantly streaming?
And the rocket's red glare, the bomb bursting in air,
Gave proof through the night that our flag was still there
    O say does that star-spangled banner yet wave
    O'er the land of the free and the home of the brave?

On the shore dimly seen through the mists of the deep,
Where the foe's haughty host in dread silence reposes,
What is that which the breeze, o'er the towering steep,
As it fitfully blows, half conceals, half discloses?
Now it catches the gleam of the morning's first beam
In full glory reflected now shines in the stream
    'Tis the star-spangled banner—O long may it **wave**
    O'er the land of the free and the home of the **brave!**

And where is that band who so vauntingly swore,
That the havoc of war and the battle's confusion
A home and a Country should leave us no more?
Their blood has wash'd out their foul footstep's **pollution**
No refuge could save the hireling and slave
From the terror of flight or the gloom of the grave,
    And the star-spangled banner in triumph doth **wave**
    O'er the land of the free and the home of the brave.

O thus be it ever when freemen shall stand
Between their lov'd home and the war's desolation!
Blest with vict'ry and peace may the heav'n rescued **land**
Praise the power that hath made and preserv'd us a **nation!**
Then conquer we must, when our cause it is just.
And this be our motto—"In God is our Trust."
    And the star-spangled banner in triumph shall wave,
    O'er the land of the free and the home of the brave.

> **OUR NATIONAL ANTHEM**
>
> A Gallup poll shows that only 31 per cent of the population actually knows the name of our national anthem.

(The Star-Spangled Banner, adopted by Congress in 1931 as the national anthem of the United States, was written by Francis Scott Key, a Baltimore lawyer, in 1814. England was at war with the United States, and Key had gone aboard a British warship to arrange the release of an American prisoner. He was forced to stay on board during the night-long bombardment of Fort McHenry near Baltimore. In great anxiety he wondered whether the fort could withstand the British attack. At daybreak, as firing ceased, Key saw the Stars and Stripes still waving. In joy and relief he wrote this great poem.)

Know America

OREGON
Lumber

CALIFORNIA
Oranges

NOR...
W...

GOOD CITIZENSHIP

IA

IOWA
Corn

TEXAS
Cattle

7. Good Citizenship in the World

Respect Those from Other Cultures

AS "WE" SEE IT

We live in a world community

Modern transportation and communication have brought nations closer and closer together; we have to work with our neighbors and get along with them. We have to *talk* with them. We and our neighbors must "speak the same language" in a sense.

Prosperity depends upon the mutually peaceful and harmonious relationship established between all countries.

It's Your World

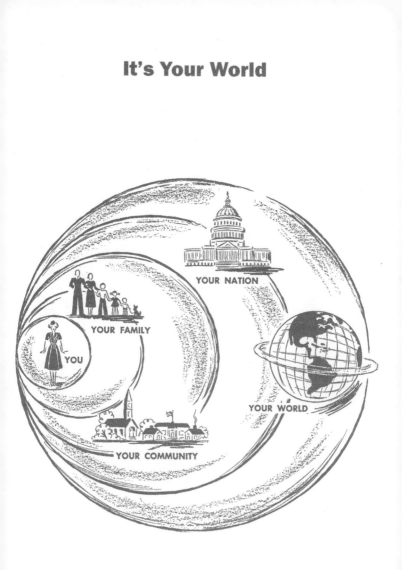

Read the newspaper

Read regularly your local paper, a good large-city newspaper, and a reliable news magazine.

See if you can find newspapers or magazines that give fair and impartial interpretation to the news of the day. Read one of these regularly.

Know Your World

A spirit of friendliness and under-standing among the peoples of the world is more important than ever for its existence.

You have your chance to meet people from all over the world at school, at church or synagogue, in your walk to the corner store, in your family and your neighbor's family. In addition, at your local library you can read about many peoples, learn their songs and dances and games, become familiar with their arts and crafts, their food, their languages.

Citizenship in the World

CITIZENSHIP IN THE WORLD

Our country is full of good citizens. And our country is a good citizen itself, because it helps other countries. The United States is by far the richest nation in the world. Many countries are so poor that many children do not have enough to eat or schools to go to. Our Government tries to help them in several ways. Here are some:

- By giving them food and services or lending money to them at little cost.

- By sending Peace Corps workers to teach in their schools; help build roads, bridges, and factories; and teach farmers the best ways to grow crops.

- By buying the things they produce and selling them things they want. (The countries help us by this trade, too.)

- By sending doctors, scientists, and engineers to work in other countries.

- By bringing students from other countries to the United States to study.

Liberty Enlightening the World

At the Ocean's gate, facing the ancient Sea, holding high the torch of Freedom, like a sentinel great and mighty, stands the Statue of Liberty, unto the world proclaiming, "My name is Liberty.   The land I guard is America. The Republic I represent is that of Freedom, Equality, Justice and Humanity, established by the Constitution of the United States."

Credits

Cover: Boy illustration from *Now and Then Stories* by M. M. Ames and Odille Ousely, illustrated by Mary Royt, Webster Publishing Co., 1945. Shield illustration from *The Constitution of The United States* booklet by James A. Moss, 1935. **Endpages:** "Steps Toward Good Citizenship," Graphics Institute, no date. **p. 1:** Illustration by James Montgomery Flagg from *What To Do For Uncle Sam* by Carolyn Sherwin Bailey, A. Flanagan Company, 1925. **p. 3:** Illustration from *The Constitution is Your Business*, Good Reading Rack Service, Inc., 1954. **pp. 4–5:** Illustration from *Now and Then Stories* by M. M. Ames and Odille Ousely, illustrated by Mary Royt, Webster Publishing Co., 1945. **pp. 6–7:** Illustration from *Merit Badge Series: Citizenship*, Boy Scouts of America, 1953, 1960. Provided courtesy Boys Scouts of America. **pp. 8–9:** Illustration from *Around the Corner* by Mabel O'Donnell and Byron H. VanRoekel, illustrated by Louis Cary and Audrey Sinnott, Harper & Row Publishers, 1966. **pp. 10–11:** Illustration from *All About Your Hair*, Charlescraft Corporation, no date. **pp. 12–13:** "A Good Citizen" from *Conduct and Citizenship* by Edwin C. Broome and Edwin W. Adams, The Macmillan Company, 1928. Illustration from *The Fabulous Future*, Good Reading Rack Service, Inc., 1955. **pp. 14–15:** "Your mental power" from *Teen Guide to Homemaking* by Marion S. Barclay and Frances Champion, illustrated by Maxine Kramer, The McGraw-Hill Book Company, 1961. Illustration from *All About Your Hair*, Charlescraft Corporation, no date. "A Well Life Promotes Good Mental Health" from *Teen-Agers: A Health And Personal Development Text for All Teen-Agers* by Gladys Gardner, W. W. Bauer, M.D., and Helen S. Shacter, illustrated by Connie Moran, Scott, Foresman and Company, 1954. Reprinted by permission of Addison-Wesley Educational Publishers, Inc. **pp. 16–17:** Illustration from *How to Play Pool*, The Burrowes Corporation, no date. Illustration from *It's Fun to Plan Your Vacation*, Reading Rack Service, Inc., 1955. "Planning for the best use of leisure" from *You And Your Community* by L. J. O'Rourke, D. C. Heath And Company, 1941. **pp. 18–19:** "A Record of Good Health" from *Health Studies* by F. M. Gregg and Hugh Grant Rowell, World Book Company, 1932. **pp. 20–21:** Illustration from *Good Citizenship Poster Cards*, Hasbro, Inc., 1968. Good Citizenship Poster Cards® is a trademark of Hasbro, Inc. ©2000 Hasbro, Inc. Used with permission. "To Avoid Catching and Spreading Infections" from *Teen Guide to Homemaking* by Marion S. Barclay and Frances Champion, illustrated by Maxine Kramer, The McGraw-Hill Book Company, 1961. "Always hold a handkerchief" from *Questions Children Ask* by Edith and Ernest Bonhivert, illustration by Edward Lafferty, Standard Education Society, Inc., 1967. "Breathe deeply of pure air" from *Conduct and Citizenship* by Edwin C. Broome and Edwin W. Adams, The Macmillan Company, 1928. **pp. 22–23:** "An excellent kind of exercise" illustration from *Health and Good Citizenship* by J. Mace Andress and W. A. Evans, Ginn And Company, 1925. "Fitness progress chart" from *Webelos Scout Book*, Boy Scouts of America, 1967, 1972. "Milk + Meat" from *Questions Children Ask* by Edith and Ernest Bonhivert, illustration by Edward Lafferty, Standard Education Society, Inc., 1967. **pp. 24–25:** Illustration from *Milk for You and Me* booklet by the National Dairy Council, 1949. "Don't Peel the Skin" from *What To Do for Uncle Sam* by Carolyn Sherwin Bailey, A. Flanagan Company, 1925. "Plenty of Meat" from *Health and Safety*, The Continental Press, Inc., no date. **pp. 26–27:** "Stretching is an excellent exercise" illustration from *Health and Good Citizenship* by J. Mace Andress and W. A. Evans, Ginn and Company, 1925. "Good Posture" from *Health and Safety*, The Continental Press, Inc., no date. **pp. 28–29:** "The Law of Self-Control" from *"Good American" Citizenship Posters* by William J. Hutchins, F. A. Owen Publishing Company, no date. "Thoughtfulness" and "Treat Others Well" from *Good Citizenship Poster Cards*. Good Citizenship Poster Cards® is a trademark of Hasbro, Inc. ©2000 Hasbro, Inc. "A good little boy never talks back" illustration from *Hayes Good Manners Posters, Set 1–Primary Grades*, illustrated by Bertha Kerr, Hayes School Publishing Co., Inc., 1957. Used by permission of Hayes School Publishing Co., Inc., © 1957. **pp. 30–31:** "The next time you are inclined to fret" from *Merit Badge Series: Citizenship*, Boy Scouts of America, 1953, 1960. Illustration from *Hayes Safety Posters: Intermediate Grades*, illustrated by Helen Hansen, Hayes School Publishing Co., Inc., 1961. Used by permission of Hayes School Publishing Co., Inc., © 1961. **pp. 32–33:** Illustration from *Learning About Our Families* by Kenneth D. Wann and Emma D. Sheehy, illustrated by Constance Heffron, Robert Allen, John C. Wonsetler, Thomas M. Park, Allyn and Bacon, Inc., 1962. Illustration from *Filter Queen* advertisement, no date. **pp. 34–35:** Illustration from "We cannot be good citizens" from *Conduct and Citizenship* by Edwin C. Broome and Edwin W. Adams, The Macmillan Company, 1928. Illustration from *Working Together* by Alta McIntire and Wilhelmina Hill, illustration by Eleanor Mill, Follett Publishing Company, 1965. "The good son or daughter" from *Conduct and Citizenship* by Edwin C. Broome and Edwin W. Adams, The Macmillan Company, 1928. **pp. 36–37:** Illustration from *Milk for You and Me* booklet, National Dairy Council, 1949. "Kindness, Truthfulness" from *You And Your Community* by L. J. O'Rourke, D. C. Heath and Company, 1941. **pp. 38–39:** Illustration from *Working Together* by Alta McIntire and Wilhelmina Hill, illustration by Tom Dunnington, Follett Publishing Company, 1965. Woman rocking illustration from *Good Citizen: The Rights and Duties of an American*, The American Heritage Foundation, 1948. **pp. 40–41:** "Special occasions the family may celebrate" from *Teen Guide to Homemaking* by Marion S. Barclay and Frances Champion, illustrated by Maxine Kramer, The McGraw-Hill Book Company, 1961. Family in car illustration from *From Bicycles to Boomerangs* by Byron H. VanRoekel and Mary Jean Kluwe, illustrated by Ed Augustiny, Bill Baker, John Henry, James Curran, Paul Hazelrigg, Bart Jerner, Robert Kresin, H. Charles McBarron, Tak Murakami, Jerry Pinkney, Don Tate, and James Teason, Harper & Row Publishers, 1966. "Outdoor activities for family fun" from *Teen Guide to Homemaking* by Marion S. Barclay and Frances Champion, The McGraw-Hill Book Company, 1961. Illustration from *Now and Then Stories* by M. M. Ames and Odille Ousely, illustrated by Mary Royt, Webster Publishing Co., 1945. **pp. 42–43:** Illustration from *What Are Vitamins?* by E. C., Medical Laboratories, Inc., 1942, 1943, and 1944. "Ideas for activities" from *Teen Guide to Homemaking* by Marion S. Barclay and Frances Champion, The McGraw-Hill Book Company, 1961. **pp. 44–45:** "Safety Checklist" from *Merit Badge Series: Citizenship*, Boy Scouts of America, 1953, 1960. "Do not play" illustration from *Questions Children Ask* by Edith and Ernest Bonhivert, illustration by Edward Lafferty, Standard Education Society, Inc., 1967. Fire illustration from *Home Protection Exercises for Your Family*, Ohio Valley Civil Defense Authority, no date. **pp. 46–47:** Vacuum illustration from Hoover Company, no date. "Things that must be done regularly" and "Things that must be done occasionally" from *Teen Guide to Homemaking* by Marion S. Barclay and Frances Champion, The McGraw-Hill

Book Company, 1961. Grocery illustration from *Learning About Our Families* by Kenneth D. Wann and Emma D. Sheehy, illustrated by Constance Heffron, Robert Allen, John C. Wonsetler, Thomas M. Park, Allyn and Bacon, Inc., 1962. **pp. 48–49:** Illustration from *Visualized Civics* by Charles E. Perry and William E. Buckley, Oxford Book Company, Inc., 1962. "The urge to get more" from *Visualized Civics* by Charles E. Perry and William E. Buckley, Oxford Book Company, Inc., 1962. **pp. 50–51:** Illustration from *Learning About Our Families* by Kenneth D. Wann and Emma D. Sheehy, illustrated by Constance Heffron, Robert Allen, John C. Wonsetler, Thomas M. Park, Allyn and Bacon, Inc., 1962. **pp. 52–53:** "Advantages of education" illustration from *Visualized Civics* by Charles E. Perry and William E. Buckley, Oxford Book Company, Inc., 1962. "In your school" from *Visualized Civics* by Charles E. Perry and William E. Buckley, Oxford Book Company, Inc., 1962. Illustration and "Hints for good school citizenship" from *English In Action* by J. C. Tressler and Henry I. Christ, Illustrated by Richard C. Bartlett, Jr., Josephine Cole, Barbara Corrigan, Hazel Hoecker, Galina Ignatieff, Wyncie King, Robert MacLean, John Nielsen, Catherine Scholz, and Don Sibley, D. C. Heath and Company, 1955. **pp. 54–55:** Illustration from *Good Citizenship Poster Cards*, Hasbro, 1968. Good Citizenship Poster Cards® is a trademark of Hasbro, Inc. ©2000 Hasbro, Inc. Used with permission. "The law of clean play" from *"Good American" Citizenship Posters* by William J. Hutchins, F. A. Owen Publishing Company, no date. "A good school citizen" from *Citizenship Through Problems* by J. B. Edmonson and A. Dondineau, The Macmillan Company, no date. **pp. 56–57:** Illustration from *Sharing Ideas* by Thomas Clark Pollock and J. Harold Straub, illustrated by Eleanor Dart and Violet LaMont, The Macmillan Company, 1954, 1960. **pp. 58–59:** "The businessman should play fair" from *Elementary Community Civics* by R. O. Hughes, Allyn and Bacon, 1932. Illustration from *Develop Your Leadership Potential* by Shon Ross, Employee Communications, Inc., 1976. **pp. 60–61:** "The intelligent business head" from *Principles of Hygiene*, The Government of the Province of Quebec, 1920. Illustration from *Now and Then Stories* by M. M. Ames and Odille Ousley, illustrated by Mary Royt, Webster Publishing Co., 1945. **pp. 62–63:** Illustration from International Correspondence Schools advertisement, no date. Typing illustration from *The Day I Was Proudest to Be an American*, Good Reading Rack Service, Inc., 1959. "I must be honest" from *Conduct and Citizenship* by Edwin C. Broome and Edwin W. Adams, The Macmillan Company, 1928. **pp. 64–65:** Illustration from *Home Protection Exercises for Your Family*, Ohio Valley Civil Defense Authority, no date. "The law of teamwork" from *"Good American" Citizenship Posters* by William J. Hutchins, F. A. Owen Publishing Company, no date. **pp. 66–67:** Illustration from *Learning About Our Families* by Kenneth D. Wann and Emma D. Sheehy, illustrated by Constance Heffron, Robert Allen, John C. Wonsetler, Thomas M. Park, Allyn and Bacon, Inc., 1962. **pp. 68–69:** Illustration from *In The Neighborhood* by Paul R. Hanna and Genevieve Anderson Hoyt, illustrated by Jack White, Scott, Foresman and Company, 1958. Reprinted by permission of Addison-Wesley Educational Publishers, Inc. "The Pilgrim Fathers" from *Good Citizen: The Rights and Duties of an American*, The American Heritage Foundation, 1948. Illustration from *In The Neighborhood* by Paul R. Hanna and Genevieve Anderson Hoyt, illustrated by Jack White, Scott, Foresman and Company, 1958. Reprinted by permission of Addison-Wesley Educational Publishers, Inc. **pp. 70–71:** Illustration from *English in Action* by J. C. Tressler and Henry I. Christ, illustrated by Richard C. Bartlett, Jr., Josephine Cole, Barbara Corrigan, Hazel Hoecker, Galina Ignatieff, Wyncie King, Robert MacLean, John Nielsen, Catherine Scholz, and Don Sibley, D. C. Heath And Company, 1955. Shaking hands illustration from *Teen Guide to Homemaking* by Marion S. Barclay and Frances Champion, illustrated by Maxine Kramer, The McGraw-Hill Book Company, 1961. "In order to be a desirable member" from *You and Your Community* by L. J. O'Rourke, D. C. Heath And Company, 1941. **pp. 72–73:** Tend to your home illustration from *Home*, Fidelity Federal Savings & Loan Association, April 1960. Illustrations from *How to Paint*, Sears, Roebuck and Co. booklet, no date. "Rake up the straw" from *What To Do for Uncle Sam* by Carolyn Sherwin Bailey, A. Flanagan Company, 1925. **pp. 74–75:** Illustration from *The Amy Vanderbilt Success Program for Women: HOW TO HELP YOUR HUSBAND GET AHEAD* (page 24) by Nina Fisher; illustrations by Frank Lacano; © 1964 by Nelson Doubleday Inc. Used by special permission of BOOKSPAN. "Signs of blight" from *Thresholds to Adult Living* by Hazel Thompson Craig, Chas A. Bennett Co., Inc., 1962. "Street lighting" from *Elementary Community Civics* by R. O. Hughes, Allyn and Bacon, 1932. Illustration from *English In Action* by J. C. Tressler and Henry I. Christ, illustrated by Richard C. Bartlett, Jr., Josephine Cole, Barbara Corrigan, Hazel Hoecker, Galina Ignatieff, Wyncie King, Robert MacLean, John Nielsen, Catherine Scholz, and Don Sibley, D. C. Heath And Company, 1955. **pp. 76–77:** Illustration from *Questions Children Ask* by Edith and Ernest Bonhivert, illustration by George Okomoto, Standard Education Society, Inc., 1967. **pp. 78–79:** "It is not right to leave poison" from *What To Do For Uncle Sam* by Carolyn Sherwin Bailey, A. Flanagan Company, 1925. Illustration from *Just for Fun* by Guy L. Bond, Grace A. Dorsey, Marie C. Cuddy, and Kathleen Wise, illustrated by Gladys Turley Mitchell, Lyons and Carnahan, 1956. Illustration from *In the Neighborhood* by Paul R. Hanna and Genevieve Anderson Hoyt, illustrated by Jack White, Scott, Foresman and Company, 1958. Reprinted by permission of Addison-Wesley Educational Publishers, Inc. **pp. 80–81:** Illustration from *Hayes Good Manners Posters, Set 1–Primary Grades*, illustrated by Bertha Kerr, Hayes School Publishing Co., Inc., 1957. Used by permission of Hayes School Publishing Co., Inc., © 1957. **pp. 82–83:** Illustration from *It's Fun to Plan Your Vacation*, Good Reading Rack Service, Inc., 1955. "Names of Parts" illustration from *Junior Rifle Handbook*, National Rifle Association, 1960. **pp. 84–85:** Illustration from *Learning About Our Families* by Kenneth D. Wann and Emma D. Sheehy, illustrated by Constance Heffron, Robert Allen, John C. Wonsetler, Thomas M. Park, Allyn and Bacon, Inc., 1962. **pp. 86–87:** "A Heart for Hospitality" from *Good Citizen: The Rights and Duties of an American*, The American Heritage Foundation, 1948. Illustration from *The Amy Vanderbilt Success Program for Women: HOW TO HELP YOUR HUSBAND GET AHEAD* (page 53) by Nina Fisher, illustrations by Frank Lacano; © 1964 by Nelson Doubleday Inc. Used by special permission of BOOKSPAN. "Remember: the same conduct" from *Conduct and Citizenship* by Edwin C. Broome and Edwin W. Adams, The Macmillan Company, 1928. **pp. 88–89:** Illustration from *Principles of Hygiene*, The Government of the Province of Quebec, 1920. "In every community" from *Elementary Community Civics* by R. O. Hughes, Allyn and Bacon, 1932. **pp. 90–91:** Illustration from *In the Neighborhood* by Paul R. Hanna and Genevieve

Anderson Hoyt, illustrated by Jack White, Scott, Foresman and Company, 1958. Reprinted by permission of Addison-Wesley Educational Publishers, Inc. "What one community found" illustration from *Citizenship Through Problems* by J. B. Edmonson and A. Dondineau, The Macmillan Company, no date. **pp. 92-93:** Illustration from *In the Neighborhood* by Paul R. Hanna and Genevieve Anderson Hoyt, illustrated by Jack White, Scott, Foresman and Company, 1958. Reprinted by permission of Addison-Wesley Educational Publishers, Inc. "Wherever people act" from *Visualized Civics* by Charles E. Perry and William E. Buckley, Oxford Book Company, Inc., 1962. "The views and feelings" from *Elementary Community Civics* by R. O. Hughes, Allyn and Bacon, 1932. **pp. 94-95:** "People are likely" from *Living in Our Communities* by Edward Krug and I. James Quillen, Scott, Foresman & Company, 1954. Illustration from *It's Fun to Plan Your Vacation*, Good Reading Rack Service, Inc., 1955. "Examples of poor community spirit" illustration from *Visualized Civics* by Charles E. Perry and William E. Buckley, Oxford Book Company, Inc., 1962. "What the community may offer" from *Teen Guide to Homemaking* by Marion S. Barclay and Frances Champion, illustrated by Maxine Kramer, The McGraw-Hill Book Company, 1961. **pp. 96-97:** Illustration from *Visualized Civics* by Charles E. Perry and William E. Buckley, Oxford Book Company, Inc., 1962. "Remember that the best way" from *Conduct and Citizenship* by Edwin C. Broome and Edwin W. Adams, The Macmillan Company, 1928. Illustration from *In the Neighborhood* by Paul R. Hanna and Genevieve Anderson Hoyt, illustrated by Jack White, Scott, Foresman and Company, 1958. Reprinted by permission of Addison-Wesley Educational Publishers, Inc. "Sin: an oath" from *Elementary Community Civics* by R. O. Hughes, Allyn and Bacon, 1932. **pp. 98-99:** "How to plant a tree" illustration from *Senior Girl Scouting*, illustrated by Jean Calhnou, Girl Scouts of the U.S.A., 1952. Reprinted by permission of Girl Scouts of the U.S.A. Illustration from *Health and Safety*, The Continental Press, Inc., no date. **pp. 100-101:** Illustration from *Good Citizenship Poster Cards*, 1968. Good Citizenship Poster Cards® is a trademark of Hasbro, Inc. ©2000 Hasbro, Inc. Used with permission. Illustration from *You and Your Community* by L. J. O'Rourke, D. C. Heath and Company, 1941. "The safety of the community" from *You and Your Community* by L. J. O'Rourke, D. C. Heath and Company, 1941. **pp. 102-103:** "The Life You Save" from *Welcome to the Highway*, The Goodyear Tire & Rubber Company, 1964. **pp. 104-105:** Illustration from The Constitution is Your Business, Reading Rack Service, Inc., 1954. **pp. 106-107:** "Cigarettes or a better community" from *You and Your Community* by L. J. O'Rourke, D. C. Heath and Company, 1941. "Taxes are a way to share" from *Living in Our Communities* by Edward Krug and I. James Quillen, Scott, Foresman & Company, 1954. Illustration from *You and Your Community* by L. J. O'Rourke, D. C. Heath and Company, 1941. **pp. 108-109:** "So you're going to vote" illustration from *Good Citizen: The Rights and Duties of an American*, The American Heritage Foundation, 1948. "The very first duty" from *Visualized Civics* by Charles E. Perry and William E. Buckley, Oxford Book Company, Inc., 1962. "Many people feel their vote" from *Thresholds to Adult Living* by Hazel Thompson Craig, Chas A. Bennett Co., Inc., 1962. "These marks are legal" illustration from *Good Citizen: The Rights and Duties of an American*, The American Heritage Foundation, 1948. **pp. 110-111:** "When you receive a notice" from *Good Citizen: The Rights and Duties of an American*, The American Heritage Foundation, 1948. Illustration from *Good Citizen: The Rights and Duties of an American*, The American Heritage Foundation, 1948. **pp. 112-113:** "Who Me?" from *Good Citizen: The Rights and Duties of an American*, The American Heritage Foundation, 1948. "State government" illustration from *Merit Badge Series: Citizenship*, Boy Scouts of America, 1953, 1960. Provided courtesy Boys Scouts of America. **pp. 114-115:** "Forms of address" from *Good Citizen: The Rights and Duties of an American*, The American Heritage Foundation, 1948. "Whenever you have a question" from *Good Citizen: The Rights and Duties of an American*, The American Heritage Foundation, 1948. **pp. 116-117:** "Displaying the flag" from *Good Citizen: The Rights and Duties of an American*, The American Heritage Foundation, 1948. Illustration from *This Wonderful Country of Ours* by Walter Johnson, The Stevens-Davis Company, 1946. **pp. 118-119:** "The good American" from *"Good American" Citizenship Posters* by William J. Hutchins, F. A. Owen Publishing Company, no date. "How to Register for the Draft" from *Magruder's American Government* by William A. McClenaghan, © Mary Magruder Smith, Prentice Hall, 1993. **pp. 120-121:** "Code of the Junior Rifleman" from *Junior Rifle Handbook*, National Rifle Association, 1960. "Rights and Privileges of a Citizen" by Frances Cavanah and Lloyd E. Smith. **pp. 122-123:** Illustration from *The Constitution is Your Business*, Good Reading Rack Service, Inc., 1954. "From the Constitution" from *Good Citizen: The Rights and Duties of an American*, The American Heritage Foundation, 1948. **pp. 124-125:** "The Birth of Our Flag" illustration from postcard, Asheville Post Card Co., no date. "The Star-Spangled Banner" from *Good Citizen: The Rights and Duties of an American*, The American Heritage Foundation, 1948. **pp. 126-127:** Illustration from *Game of the States*. Game of the States® is a trademark of Hasbro, Inc. ©2000 Hasbro, Inc. Used with permission. **pp. 128-129:** Illustration from *Learning About Our Families* by Kenneth D. Wann and Emma D. Sheehy, illustrated by Constance Heffron, Robert Allen, John C. Wonseller, Thomas M. Park, Allyn and Bacon, Inc., 1962. **pp. 130-131:** Illustration from *Visualized Civics* by Charles E. Perry and William E. Buckley, Oxford Book Company, Inc., 1962. **pp. 132-133:** "Modern transportation" from *Merit Badge Series: Citizenship*, Boy Scouts of America, 1953, 1960. Illustration from *Working Together* by Alta McIntire and Wilhelmina Hill, illustration by Beatrice Derwinski, Follett Publishing Company, 1965. "Prosperity depends" from *Citizenship Through Problems* by J. B. Edmonson and A. Dondineau, The Macmillan Company, no date. Illustration from *Senior Girl Scouting*, illustrated by Jean Calhnou, Girl Scouts of the U.S.A., 1952. Reprinted by permission of Girl Scouts of the USA. **pp. 134-135:** "Read regularly your local paper" from *Senior Girl Scouting*, illustrated by Jean Calhnou, Girl Scouts of the U.S.A., 1952. "A spirit of friendliness" from *Senior Girl Scouting*, illustrated by Jean Calhnou, Girl Scouts of the U.S.A., 1952. Illustrations from *Working Together* by Alta McIntire and Wilhelmina Hill, illustration by Robert Lee, Follett Publishing Company, 1965. **pp. 136-137:** "Our country is full of good citizens" from *Webelos Scout Book*, Boy Scouts of America, 1967, 1972. Provided courtesy Boys Scouts of America. "Liberty Enlightening the World" from *The Constitution of the United States* booklet by James A. Moss, 1935.